Reflection of Self

ANTHONY NEWTON

Copyright © 2022 by Anthony Newton

All rights reserved.

No portion of this book may be reproduced in any form without written permission from the publisher or author, except as permitted by U.S. copyright law.

for those who inspired me to write

Contents

1. Be Patient With Me   1
   Dinner Rhetoric
   Heartbreaker
   Where Did She Go
   Heartfelt Confusion
   Erotic Erosion
   Slipping

2. Introspective Thoughts   7
   Hope Deferred
   They Cry
   Honestly,
   Don't Leave Anymore
   Untouchable
   The Tunnel

One In the Same

3. Life's Intricate Moments   15
    Destiny's Child
    My Cup Runneth' Over
    The Learning Curve
    Sonhood
    The Places We Go
    Break The Mold
    Mustard Seed
    Faith
    The Return
    Carlin's Eyes
    Where Do We Go After We Die

Afterword   26

About Author   27

Be Patient With Me

My Heart's Essay

Dinner Rhetoric

Conversations,

Conversations about those conversations

Inner elation at seeing the beauty of my manifestation

Oh, the electricity, oh my;

You've caught my mind's eye

We ate, we conversed

So fluidly it felt rehearsed

Gliding over the waters of our lives

There were plenty of times we could have lied

Watery starts are for children,

Adults should drink wine,

Electricity like ours is uncommon to find

Yet we clearly see the origin of its flow

Lady, you've turned on a light in my mind,

Only you can determine what is shown.

Heartbreaker

The low tide reveals a shore of despair in your mind.

At one point in time, it would've been hard to find.

Scarce to see.

Because it was covered by the current of my love.

It was hidden by me.

Your heart aches.

Its call reaches my spirit.

I don't have the medicine because I caused the break,

Saw the reality coming and I feared it.

I'd only confuse you further if I tried to mend it.

You were the whole package, and still, I had nowhere to send it.

Forgive me, I have to find myself.

A journey of self discovery.

Never lose sight of your worth.

There's an even better man waiting for you after recovery.

I just wish I could have made it work.

Where Did She Go

Love, she's gone.

Where did she go?

When did she leave?

Was it from a lack of expression, or opportunity?

Were we not prepared mentally?

I blamed you, and you blamed me.

Though in retrospect I am able to see,

Love left because of us.

We made her leave, forced her out onto the street.

Our arguments collected together like the writings of a corpus.

The toxic symphony of our opus.

Unbearable to Love's ears.

Unable to survive in those conditions.

Her essence became lost over the years.

What was behind all of the tension?

Miscommunication?

We'll never know unless we mention,

That we took love for granted.

Heartfelt Confusion

To me, it never occurred,

That what I gave you could never be returned.

Yet I'd do it once more, if I was able.

You held on to the love I gave you.

The love you gifted me, I burned.

I couldn't keep it.

Getting rid of it kept me stable.

I never realized my own well of love was dry,

Not until I tried to share my water with another.

Oceanic covers, the way thoughts of you blanket my conscious.

No matter how hard I try to understand,

I'll never be able to grasp the nonsense.

REFLECTION OF SELF

Erotic Erosion

The euphoria of the first time,

Never to be felt again.

Love and lust over what was mine,

Like all things, it's pleasures fated to end.

No longer attracted to the body, the mind, or even the spirit.

This feeling of nothingness, I see why others fear it.

What is life without love?

A blank canvas.

Because like an artist without a muse,

A life devoid of love lacks color.

Slipping

Watch your step.

If you fall again,

If you fall again you won't rise from it.

Can't afford another intimate mistake,

The last, it was costly,

The toll it took, you still pay.

Everyday.

You're losing your balance.

Dense emotions protect your heart.

A composer of love,

Your vulnerability, your compassion,

Both tools that define your art.

Her song,

The chords of her soul,

Lower your guard.

Take off your armor,

Let her see who you are.

You're falling in her direction, it's true.

If you are going to let yourself fall once more,

Just make sure, she's the one to catch you.

Introspective Thoughts

The Condition of My Reality

Hope Deferred

What happens when hope defers?

Well, take a look outside

Better yet,

Stare into the eyes of our people,

They're blind.

Death is normalized,

We tried to raise the children only after the babies died.

What happens when hope defers?

Well, our minds defer to desperation.

America's cupboards, raided by an infestation known as inflation.

What happens when the working class can no longer work?

The recession has lasted quite longer than expected,

Leave a wound open long enough and it'll end up infected.

What happens when hope defers?

So will our love for one another.

Blood relation will hold no weight.

Friend will become foe, brother will fight brother

And the devil will finally be satisfied by our hatred for each other.

What happens when hope defers?

They Cry

It's okay to cry little one.

You don't have to hold back those tears.

The trauma you've experienced cannot be undone.

An expectation of love, but they made you fear.

It is not your fault,

The blame is not your own.

Cornered by a bully, still you fought.

Beaten down by a life beyond your control.

I'm so sorry little one,

Sorry, that their shortcomings killed your innocence.

Sorry, that for each time they touched your body, it stunted the growth of your mind.

Sorry, that it all could've been prevented if someone was vigilant.

Sorry, because all I can offer you is hope, that the scars fade away with time.

Honestly,

If we're being honest

I don't like you.

Actually, I don't even know you

I remember who you used to be

I had more tolerance for the old you

"This imposter, who is he?"

Says everyone who couldn't see,

That this person that you are now,

Was always a possibility

They never paid attention to the signs,
The flashes of this personality
Unfortunately I had my doubts,
What a pain it is
To live with this reality.

Don't Leave Anymore

Why did you leave?
Don't give me the rationale,
When you left I was six,
Dad, I'm seven now.
You love me but you can't stay.
Every six months, that's what you say.
I miss you more each passing day.
Thinking, "When are we going to play?"
I hate Sam.
He's not even my real uncle.
When is he going to let you come home?
Your emails say you're heading South.
Ocean waves drown your cell phone.

Dad, I can't be the man of the house.
I don't know what I'm supposed to do.
I tried on your boots the other day,
Maybe they'll make me strong like you.

Untouchable

Leave me,
If you haven't already
Because to see me in the light,
Will offer the realization I'm dreading.
Airtight, I am confined to my despair
Your words never reach my ears,
I think that it is fair,
That way you don't see my tears.
Standing here on my last leg,
With my pride as a crutch.
I can see you but when I reach out,
Air is all I touch.

The Tunnel

It is dark.

No luminescent body could affect the brightness of the mind's environment.

Not yet pitch black, but soon enough it will reach that point.

Through stark adjustment my eyes are able to diagnose where I am.

The Tunnel.

Never have I been this hopeless, stuck between the winding corridors of sadness and helplessness.

Muffled screaming, my mind teeming with emotional distress contained by strength of will.

Still, I search for a way out.

But I've begun to lose my sense of direction, as my heart's compass demagnetizes.

"Does anyone truly care?"

The question's resounding echo overwhelms my conscience.

The tunnel becomes darker.

Lip service has become routine for me as I navigate through the tunnel.

Even a glimpse of a display of negative emotions makes others irate.

So I withhold the inclination to share the coordinates of my thoughts.

I am enveloped by the darkness of the tunnel.

One In the Same

It's quite a shame

To witness a young man

Who doesn't know his name.

Who thinks his worth,

Is determined by the contents of his purse.

Mentally mislabeled,

His understanding of self, disabled.

He deserves to eat

Yet self-deceit steals his seat at the table.

His mental state is a pure reflection of misdirection,

Allow me to explain this misconception:

With no one to affirm his good traits,

They become misconceived as mistakes,

This is the root of his self-hate.

The early decision that it is too late.

Old men, show the young man empathy,

Say to him: "I was once you, and I too, hated being me."

"Think of your life as an open sea, waves will crash at times, but you won't get through, until you, realize its beauty."

Life's Intricate Moments

Destiny's Child

Slow down,

Close your eyes

It's time to free your mind,

To let your spirit unwind

You are Destiny's child,

Birthed by fate

Each step you take

Never too early,

Never too late

The perfect maternity

For all of eternity.

Connected,

You look to the stars for hope,

They only show your reflection.

My Cup Runneth' Over

It seems consistent that each day I wake

Of my mind I wonder what they will take,

Obligations, important conversations

Their politics grasp ahold of my soul,

Evidence to support their litigation

No time to search for the unknown

A busy bee, what my mother calls me,

She voiced her discomfort over the state of my life

At the end of the road they all will see,

The reward I receive for my sacrifice.

The Learning Curve

There was a young man beside himself with emotion,

He couldn't understand his peers and the way they lived so selfishly,

Uprooting themselves to be like others,

Never realizing it was killing their own trees.

My father noticed this fallacy and sat me up on his knee,

This is what he said to me:

Can't force the thirsty to drink.

Nor can the dumb be forced to think.

You can give someone a bottle of water,

Lo' and behold they go and drink from the sink.

Wisdom must be accepted before it can be applied.

Not too many enjoy the burden of being wise

It's fun to be Young, but what will happen when you run out of time?

It's fun to be Wild but what will happen when you are put in chains?

It's fun to be Free, do as you please,

Except, freedom is financed by money.

The will of the heart is revealed in one's actions.

Wisdom is not always a part of the equation,

Some people don't like fractions.

Wisdom is not one's burden,

It's one's choice,

An extension of your voice.

Apply it exceedingly

Sonhood

"A foolish son is a grief to his father, and bitterness to her that bare him"

- Proverbs 17:25

Born innocent,

With the weight of the world on his infant spine.

No worries, the innocence and naïveté will erode with time

The circumstances of his childhood will determine his path,

But just because he wasn't born into first place, doesn't guarantee he'll come in last.

Your son is your legacy,

The bearer of the family crest.

In him is the blueprint of his forefathers,

And he must protect these sacred texts.

A good son is a good listener,

But confident enough to make his own mistakes.

He gains wisdom from each trial,

And learns from the footprint of each step he takes.

Be patient with your son,

For there are times that he will stray.

He is only testing the winds of life,

The breeze will bring him back to you one day.

Wiser and grateful he will return,

For Life is the best teacher,

Of its lessons, every man has learned.

Raised to be a King,

Every prince will soon have his day.

And the story of their lives they shall sing,

Each volume should not be the same.

But all will be united as children of the Creator.

The Places We Go

Oh, how I used to wonder about the places I'd go.

I begged to know.

I needed to know.

I just had to go.

To places where my energies could flow,

Free to make the mistake of being myself.

No one else.

No facades, yet able to become whomever I wanted.

Oh, and when I reached those places I flaunted.

A mind, with a flavor like mine, was one of a kind you see.

Soon they hated me.

Oh, the places I've been

The places I've sinned

The places I've prayed

God knew I couldn't have stayed.

I just had to go.

Break The Mold

Personal education should only stop at death.

Artists who were truly masterful inspire learning long after their last breath.

In any discipline, mastery of the heart must come before mastery of the mind.

Because emotional impulse must be refined

Before we can truly create art.

Obsession breeds consistency,

You must be okay with being misunderstood.

Plan with creativity,

Break away from conformity's dealings, its ideas are never good.

Willingness to re-educate will separate the crowd,

You can't be the master of nations, if all you're willing to know is small-town.

Mustard Seed

Two millimeters.

Two millimeters of faith is all you need.

Are you ready to sow your mustard seed?

It won't bear fruit immediately,

Or even some years down the line.

This is the leap that you will take,

Your faith should have no regard for time.

Faith

I know what you told me.

I'll never forget the dreams they sold me.

But I have faith that you'll hold me.

They fear your power.

They don't believe the possibility of the implausible.

So in degrading criticism I was showered,

They never thought I'd make it out of the crucible.

I did.

I march forth with humility and ambition.

To see my wildest dreams come to fruition.

I'm not at the round table yet, but when I get there,

I'll make sure that all who are moved by their faith sit there.

The Return

The fall from grace

The loss of favor

The torment of failure

The ridicule from peers

The depression

The grind

The growth

The confidence

The mastery

The return

Carlin's Eyes

I realize that there is danger in their lies.

When did they become the dictators of all lives?

They played on our shallow desire to be "free,"

But like all other commodities, "Freedom" costs a fee.

Freedom is not real. It does not exist.

If you'd open your eyes you'd see for yourself,

Thinking to which, they've trained our minds to resist.

Freedom is billed directly from life's checking.

Who collects the payment?

Rational ignorance keeps us from asking the question.

Identify your enemy, know them by name.

Do not wait until it is too late for change.

Their goal is to have you usurped of your rights.

Knowing this, you still sleep softly at night.

But maybe that's the key! Maybe that's it!

Maybe, it's called the American Dream because you have to be asleep to believe it.

Where Do We Go After We Die

Is the end really the end?

Or does death conclude the opening act?

Is an eternity of blankness all we can comprehend?

Quite sad it is,

To have lived a life of light, only to fade to black.

After I've climbed Heaven's stairway, does God wait for me at the Gates?

Or must I wait, in Purgatory amongst the 'unholy' while the sinful expiate?

Will I be reborn as a slave to atone for choices I made?

Karma is unforgiving yet fair, will Allah save me from her snare?

Is Heaven just a reflection of our own reality,

Wishfully distorted by our own principalities?

Critical thought is at the heart of my questions,

REFLECTION OF SELF

As there lies a conflict between each prophets' message.

Still, someday I expect to be judged for my life's actions.

Despite religion's varying ideas of when and how it should happen.

Afterword

The best and worst moments of my young life are inscribed onto these pages. Please treat them with care. I hope that there is a passage in here that spoke life unto you, and I am truly appreciative of the connection we have made. Take care, until next time.

Anthony

About Author

Anthony Newton, at the time of writing, is a fourth-year college student pursuing a degree in computer science.

Made in the USA
Columbia, SC
12 October 2024

43491036R00020